The Dragons of Pan Gu

Written by Kevin White

Illustrated by Rex White

For Selina and Bodhi

The Dragons of Pan Gu by Kevin White
Illustrated by Rex White
Copyright © 2013 (text) Kevin White, (illustrations) Rex White

Published by:
Chimeric Press
5299 Rau Road
West Branch, MI 48661
www.chimericpress.com
ISBN: 978-0-9847122-6-7
LCCN: 2013903745
Printed in the United States of America
by Signature Book Printing Inc., Gaithersburg, MD
First Edition: April 2013

Long ago, Pan Gu walked in the void of the heavens.

He was all there was,

and he was alone,

so Pan Gu never smiled.

"I will create a seed of seeds," he thought, "and from that my joy will grow."
He felt the forming of it in his mind, so he labored through a thought and a time,
and before the second time could pass he reached into the void and formed the seed.

"I will call it Earth," he said, and then he placed it in the heavens.

"The Earth will need a source of power," he thought, "or it will not grow."

So he reached deep down into the void and gathered his knowledge and logic,

and formed...

the black dragon.

As the black dragon flew across the Earth's sky,
she drew behind her a cloak of darkness
that smothered all it touched.

Her breath was frost and snow,
and the beating of her dark wings blew bitter winds

that froze everything it touched.

The Earth's surface remained barren.

Pan Gu frowned and called the dragon to his side.

Pan Gu was still and quiet for a moment and an age,

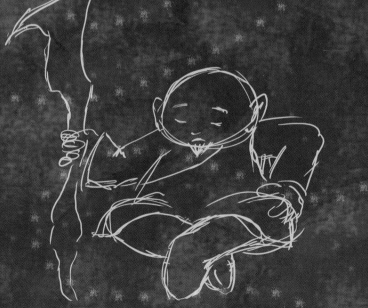

and then he reached up high into the void and gathered his ideas and dreams,

and formed...

the white dragon.

As the white dragon flew across the Earth's sky,
he shone before him a pure light that penetrated
all it touched.

His breath was smoke and fire,
and the beating of his white wings
blew scorching winds

that burned everything it touched.

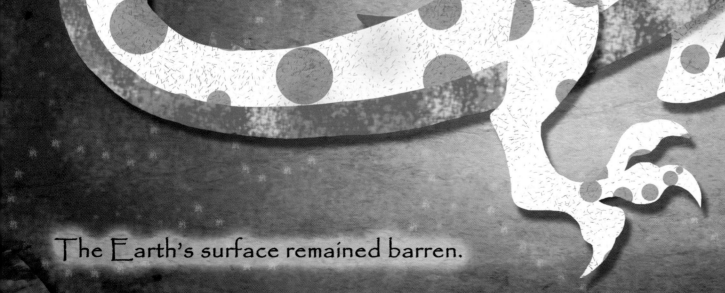

The Earth's surface remained barren.

Pan Gu frowned and called the dragon to his side.

The dragons did not get along.

Darkness chased the light
which then chased the darkness in return.

They fought tooth and claw,

and caused chaos in the void
as each tried to put an end
to the other.

When the white blazed the brightest and appeared to be winning, shadows flitted defiantly.

When the black cast her darkest cloak,
darts of light shot through holes chewed in battle.

Both dragons tried to convince Pan Gu to banish the other.

Their fighting never stopped,
and it never slowed.
The struggle for power continued
as control flowed from one to the other
and then back again.

Pan Gu realized that neither dragon could win,
and so he reached a decision. He took both dragons

and bound them to the Earth.

Their roaring shook time itself!

Their teeth and claws nearly pulled the Earth in two.

They began chasing each other
around and around

until the Earth itself began to spin.

It became neither too hot, or cold;

too light, or dark;

too wet, or dry;

and so the Earth began to grow.

The Earth grew for an eon and a day,
until one morning a small boy
stood next to his grandfather
at the edge of the ocean

and watched the sunrise
as they fished in the surf.

"There is wisdom in the balance between light and dark, ocean and land, even dreams and logic," said the Grandfather.

"Each controls for a time,
but must give way to the other
for its own sake."

"What about young and old, Grandfather?" the boy asked,
looking wistfully at the pole.

"Yes," the old man mused
as he handed the pole to the boy,
"I suppose especially then."